Bev Aisbett, a trained counsellor, is the author and illustrator of 17 highly regarded self-help books for sufferers of anxiety and depression, most notably the national bestsellers *Living with It: A Survivor's Guide to Panic Attacks* and *Taming the Black Dog: A Guide to Overcoming Depression*. These titles are distributed to health professionals nationwide and have been sold in English in the UK, US and Canada. In total, her books have been published in eight languages, selling more than half a million copies worldwide.

Bev developed a unique recovery program, The Art of Anxiety workshop, designed to educate people about anxiety and provide them with the tools with which to build their own recovery, just as Bev herself has done. Launched in 1998, this program has guided thousands of people in the 'art' of effectively managing anxiety and related conditions.

She is also a recognised artist, and her soulful paintings have been regularly exhibited in Victoria and Tasmania.

For more information and anxiety resources:
bevaisbettartofanxiety.com

BY BEV AISBETT

Living IT Up

Letting IT Go

Get Real

Taming the Black Dog

The Little Book of IT

Fixing IT

Recovery: A Journey to Healing

The Book of IT

Get Over IT

I Love Me

All of IT: A Memoir

Living with IT

30 Days 30 Ways to Overcome Anxiety

30 Days 30 Ways to Overcome Depression

Worry-Proofing Your Anxious Child

Cruising Through Calamity

The Book of Burnout

THE BOOK OF BURN OUT

WHAT IT IS. WHY IT HAPPENS. WHO GETS IT.
AND HOW TO STOP IT
BEFORE IT STOPS YOU!

BEV AISBETT

HarperCollins*Publishers*

HarperCollins*Publishers*
Australia • Brazil • Canada • France • Germany • Holland • India
Italy • Japan • Mexico • New Zealand • Poland • Spain • Sweden
Switzerland • United Kingdom • United States of America

HarperCollins acknowledges the Traditional Custodians
of the land upon which we live and work, and pays respect
to Elders past and present.

First published in Australia in 2023
by HarperCollins*Publishers* Australia Pty Limited
Gadigal Country
Level 19, 201 Elizabeth Street, Sydney NSW 2000
ABN 36 009 913 517
harpercollins.com.au

A catalogue record for this book is available from the National Library of Australia

ISBN 978 1 4607 6213 4 (paperback)
ISBN 978 1 4607 1494 2 (ebook)
ISBN 978 1 4607 4490 1 (audiobook)

Cover and internal illustrations by Bev Aisbett
Cover design by HarperCollins Design Studio
Typeset in Brandon Grotesque by Kelli Lonergan

Printed and bound by CPI Group (UK) Ltd, Croydon, CR0 4YY

DEDICATION

To all my fellow Type As – may you find peace
and have a good night's sleep.

Special thanks to Angelo Madrid for his
fabulous work finalising my doodles!

CONTENTS

INTRODUCTION

I have a CONFESSION to make – for the first time in the past thirty years of writing my books, I asked for an extension to complete this book, ironically, because of BURNOUT!

I have often joked that my books are written from LIVED EXPERIENCE, but this was taking the PERSONAL research a little too far!

I had taken on too much at one time and, as is my tendency, OVERESTIMATED my ability to get everything done in the time I had available.

This is a classic set-up for BURNOUT, where we think we can do the IMPOSSIBLE at the cost of our wellbeing, health and quality of life.

The important message from this personal example is that I knew early enough when to call it quits but, sadly, many people don't. This book is created with those people in mind.

Although the term is often casually TOSSED ABOUT, burnout is NO JOKE – it can impact every area of your life and leave you depleted in almost every sense.

And BURNOUT is COMPLEX – as I discovered when researching this book. In fact, the more I delved into BURNOUT, the more TENTACLES it grew!

So, from LOW-LEVEL burnout to the FULL-BLOWN version – and what to do about it – welcome to THE BOOK OF BURNOUT!

PART I

The HEAT is ON

CHAPTER 1

Is something BURNING?

Does your AVERAGE day look like THIS?

THE MOMENT YOU WAKE, YOU'RE 'ON' TILL BEDTIME.

YOU GRAB SOMETHING TO EAT ON THE RUN.

IF YOU GET ANY EXERCISE, YOU CRAM IN A HIGH-INTENSITY WORKOUT.

YOU MUST BE CONSTANTLY AVAILABLE.

AND EVEN 'RELAXATION' MEANS BINGEING SO YOU DON'T MISS OUT!

You're too WIRED to sleep and too TIRED to function, but you repeat this day AGAIN and AGAIN and AGAIN!

If this goes ON, you could soon be in BURNOUT!

And you're RIGHT!

DEFINING burnout is not as straightforward as it may seem at first and is NOT LIMITED to a particular WALK OF LIFE OR LIFESTYLE.

Well, I'd say it's when you've reached your LIMIT!

But is that BURNOUT or FRUSTRATION?

Could it be DEPRESSION?

or FATIGUE?

or even BOREDOM?

And how do you know when you HAVE reached your LIMIT?

Is it when you're EXHAUSTED but CARRY ON?

Or when you've reached the point where you simply CAN'T carry on?

Ask a group of people and you'll find each person has a different take on what BURNOUT means:

Interestingly, prior to 1974, there wasn't a recognised NAME for burnout, even though the condition has surely existed throughout history.

Psychologist Herbert Freudenberger and Professor of Psychology Christina Maslach first independently researched and made known the concept of BURNOUT.

Freudenberger is credited with coining the term while working long hours at a substance abuse clinic. At the time, 'burnout' was used as SLANG to describe the effects of extreme drug use, but was soon adopted by the clinic staff to describe the TOLL visited upon them by the punishing DEMANDS of their work.

Previously, BURNOUT was not recognised as a condition on its own, but was incorporated into the broader categories of 'stress syndromes' or 'nervous breakdowns'. According to the World Health Organization (W.H.O.), burnout is not regarded as a MEDICAL condition and only marginally as a MENTAL ailment.

It is only recently (2019) that W.H.O. acknowledged burnout at ALL, categorising it as 'a syndrome conceptualised as resulting from chronic WORKPLACE stress that has not been successfully managed' in the organisation's diagnostic manual, *International Classification of Diseases*.

This definition was guided by Christina Maslach's *Inventory of Burnout*, which covers three main areas:

- EXHAUSTION measures feelings of being overextended and exhausted by your work.

- CYNICISM measures an indifference or distant attitude towards your work.

- PROFESSIONAL EFFICACY measures your satisfaction with past and present accomplishments, and it explicitly assesses your expectations of continued effectiveness at work.

Again, the focus here is on WORKPLACE burnout.

In fact, W.H.O. goes on to state that 'burnout refers specifically to phenomena in the OCCUPATIONAL context and should not be applied to describe EXPERIENCES in other areas of life'.

While W.H.O.'s definition recognises one aspect of burnout (in the WORKPLACE), it disregards the various types associated with MANY aspects of living in the current climate – especially given the ADDITIONAL stresses that COVID-19 has brought to bear.

BURNOUT can affect ANYONE, from stressed-out career-driven people and celebrities to overworked employees and homemakers.

So, to DEFINE burnout, TYPES as well as DEGREES of burnout need to be considered – not only in the WORKPLACE but also in a BROADER CONTEXT, which we will explore in this book.

But in the MEANTIME, people generally agree that BURNOUT means the following:

We'll look at that NEXT.

CHAPTER 2

SAUTÉED
or
DEEP-FRIED?

As we have seen, BURNOUT is most commonly associated with the WORKPLACE, or when a person takes on extra RESPONSIBILITY and feels OVERWORKED, OVERBOOKED and INDISPENSABLE – but burnout is far more NUANCED than just being busy or overwhelmed by responsibilities.

If we return to the World Health Organization's 2019 classification of burnout – *a syndrome that results from chronic workplace stress that's not successfully managed* – again, we see the focus is on the WORKPLACE, but anyone who has lived through the last few years can testify that BURNOUT is more far-reaching and diverse in its impact than the above definition.

COVID BURNOUT is REAL and it could be said that it is as much a PANDEMIC as the physical version, affecting an entire population regardless of whether or not they are in the OFFICE (even – or especially – if that office is at HOME!).

We'll explore COVID BURNOUT later on, but it is clear from this example that there are MANY WAYS to burn out.

Let's take a look at a few situations.

OVER IT

Something that was once PLEASURABLE now holds little joy because of OVEREXPOSURE.

DONE TO DEATH

Repeating something too often until it becomes a CHORE.

UNFINISHED BUSINESS

Starting ONE thing then moving on to ANOTHER before the FIRST one is finished. Too many 'irons in the fire' lead to stress over UNCOMPLETED tasks.

PUSH, PUSH, PUSH

This type of BURNOUT can arise from a VICIOUS CYCLE of feeding off ADRENALINE.

You're DOG-TIRED but you keep PUSHING on and can't seem to STOP.

SUPERHERO SYNDROME

You make yourself INDISPENSABLE and so you become that. You are always 'ON CALL' and can never REST.

PLAGUED BY FOMO
(Fear of Missing Out)

This means exhausting yourself by trying to KEEP UP with current TRENDS or fit in with the STATUS QUO.

BORED STIFF

We often associate burnout with working TOO MUCH, but it can also happen when you're NOT CHALLENGED or feel just plain BORED. (More about this in CHAPTER 9: TOO DARN HOT.)

TAKEN TO THE LIMIT

It's all more than you can HANDLE. The DEMANDS on you have outweighed the RESOURCES you have to deal with them.

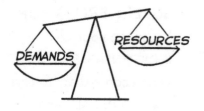

On this last point, it is important to note that everyone has a different TIPPING POINT. One person may be able to keep going far beyond someone else's LIMIT. We'll see why, later.

CHAPTER 3

Are you COOKED yet?

So how can I TELL whether or not I'm in BURNOUT?

Unfortunately, experts don't always agree on what burnout actually is. As a CONSEQUENCE, burnout is not readily or easily RECOGNISED or DIAGNOSED as a HEALTH ISSUE.

As a result, it is often left up to the INDIVIDUAL to ASSESS whether what they are experiencing is BURNOUT or not.

There are three MAIN SYMPTOMS attributed to BURNOUT:

- Feelings of ENERGY DEPLETION or EXHAUSTION

- NEGATIVITY or CYNICISM towards your situation

- REDUCED EFFICACY

I'm feeling quite DEPRESSED.
Is that the SAME as BURNOUT?

There is a difference between the feelings of OVERWHELM you may experience in BURNOUT and the negative feelings associated with DEPRESSION.

With BURNOUT, most of the negative feelings and sensations you are experiencing relate to a SPECIFIC situation. They will be eased by addressing the PRESSURES associated with being in that SITUATION (for instance, by taking time off from work).

In DEPRESSION, negative thoughts and feelings tend to focus on ALL areas of life and include LOW SELF-ESTEEM, HOPELESSNESS and often SUICIDAL IDEATIONS, so 'taking a break' may not be a solution (and may actually EXACERBATE the depression). If you feel this way, you should seek SPECIALISED CARE from a TRAINED PROFESSIONAL.

If you don't make changes to the situation that is causing your BURNOUT, however, you may SET YOURSELF UP for depression.

PHYSICAL ILLNESS or certain MEDICATIONS can cause symptoms such as FATIGUE.

Before you conclude that you have BURNOUT, explore other POSSIBLE CAUSES for your tiredness with your DOCTOR first.

But a STRESSFUL LIFESTYLE, typical of those with BURNOUT, can put people under EXTREME PRESSURE to the point of EXHAUSTION.

Exhaustion is a NORMAL reaction to STRESS – it is not necessarily a sign of DISEASE, but feeling stressed all the time is NOT NORMAL or HEALTHY!

Feeling EXHAUSTED is simply your body's way of telling you that SOMETHING has to CHANGE.

However, it is more likely that someone will be well into BURNOUT before they come to that realisation.

Too many people hit ROCK BOTTOM before they acknowledge things have gone too far.

You can turn burnout around if you RECOGNISE the SIGNS early enough – this is what we'll look at next.

In the meantime, it's time to take a moment for a little SELF-ASSESSMENT.

Has it become NORMAL for you to feel STRESSED?

Are you constantly EXHAUSTED but can't seem to take a BREAK?

Do you feel that you are tied to a situation requiring SELF-SACRIFICE?

Do you feel that you have NO CHOICE but to be AVAILABLE?

Do you think that NO-ONE else can do things as well as YOU?

Are you operating from ABSOLUTES?

Do you act as if you are INVINCIBLE? ...

... or that your own HEALTH and WELLBEING are of SECONDARY importance?

If you have answered YES to these questions, you are very likely to put yourself into BURNOUT.

But that's just LIFE, isn't it?

I can't STEP AWAY from my RESPONSIBILITIES!

Of course, but to what DEGREE? Are you sacrificing your WELLBEING for an idea of DUTY?

Overwork and stress aren't BADGES of HONOUR – they're signs that you're doing TOO MUCH.

Burnout is insidious because it tends to CREEP UP on you. It's not a matter of being FINE one day and BURNED OUT the next!

NOTE: it is POSSIBLE to burn yourself out on a TEMPORARY basis (such as organising an EVENT), but in this case, the burnout is likely to be PASSING rather than an ONGOING condition.

There are plenty of WARNING SIGNS, including PHYSICAL, MENTAL and EMOTIONAL symptoms, which we will explore shortly. But first, it's important to recognise the STAGES of burnout.

CHAPTER 4

The
SLOW
BURN

Let's take a look at how BURNOUT can slowly (but surely) TAKE OVER.

STAGE 1: HONEYMOON PHASE

Hey, not a PROBLEM. I can DO THIS!

At first, it can feel like you're moving in the RIGHT DIRECTION.

No matter your point of FOCUS – whether it's a WORK-RELATED, PHILANTHROPIC or PERSONAL pursuit – you feel up to the task and DETERMINED to see it through.

And you may well be on the RIGHT TRACK – until you start to take on TOO MUCH!

STAGE 2: JUSTIFICATION

At this stage, things on your 'TO DO' list begin to PILE UP. You start straying from your original JOB DESCRIPTION or initial GOAL.

This might involve taking on EXTRA TASKS, staying back later or agreeing to do 'FAVOURS'. You might also have not really CONSIDERED or REALISED at the outset how DEMANDING the task is that you've taken on.

However, you CONVINCE yourself that you can MANAGE – you just need to make ADJUSTMENTS. After all, what's a little DISCOMFORT when what you're doing is so IMPORTANT?

STAGE 3: MARTYRDOM

At this stage, whatever you have COMMITTED to is starting to TAKE OVER. You begin to make SACRIFICES for the sake of SEEING IT THROUGH.

These may include FAMILY TIME, SOCIAL ACTIVITIES, RELATIONSHIPS, HOBBIES and TIME TO YOURSELF.

Even worse, you start SACRIFICING things that help your WELLBEING, such as REST, SLEEP, HEALTHY EATING, EXERCISE, SELF-CARE and PERSONAL PLEASURES.

STAGE 4: CREEPING DISSATISFACTION

You start to DREAD having to put in an APPEARANCE. Something that was once STIMULATING now feels like a CHORE. You feel UNMOTIVATED and DISTRACTED.

You may have a subtle GUT FEELING that something's not right, but you write this off as 'That's just the way life is.' You think it's the SITUATION that's not right, instead of recognising that YOU aren't right in this situation.

STAGE 5: BLAME

Now, RESENTMENT is beginning to build. You feel BURDENED and OVERWHELMED. This is not what you SIGNED UP for!

You start to blame OUTSIDE FACTORS for putting you in this position – you blame your JOB, your BOSS, the person you are CARING for or your PASTIME (that has now become a BURDEN) for making you feel this way.

STAGE 6: ENVY

You look around you – no-one else seems to be having such a HARD TIME!

You may even be ACCOMMODATING someone else's ENJOYMENT while you do the SUFFERING!

By this stage, you are starting to make MISTAKES – you're less EFFICIENT, CLUMSIER and more FORGETFUL.

However, you put this down to 'having a bad day' even though, lately, most of your days have been 'BAD DAYS'. You might start to BLAME others for your own mistakes as a way of COPING because you HATE making mistakes, don't you?

STAGE 7: CONSCIOUSLY UNCONSCIOUS

At this point, you're AWARE you're not doing well but you find ways to BLOCK the EXHAUSTION, IRRITABILITY and UNWELLNESS from your consciousness.

After all, acknowledging that you're NOT COPING is a sign of FAILURE – and you don't 'do' failure, do you?

To get through, you will tend to adopt behaviours that FURTHER undermine your wellbeing because you have reached a level of complete DISREGARD for yourself. These behaviours might include UNHEALTHY EATING (such as sweet 'TREATS' or FAST FOOD), DRINKING or pushing yourself even HARDER in a kind of FRENZY.

You figure you can't REST anyway, so you may as well keep going till you DROP!

STAGE 8: TOAST

That's IT, I'm DONE!

When you've reached this point, you can no longer KID yourself that you can GO ON.

Your BODY and/or MIND will tell you – in no uncertain terms – that you are in COMPLETE and TOTAL BURNOUT.

Your BODY will do this by causing you to COLLAPSE, develop a CHRONIC ILLNESS or – even worse – have a HEART ATTACK!

Your MIND will tell you things have gone too far by breaking down – through either PANIC ATTACKS, ANXIETY or DEPRESSION.

Do you WANT to get to this stage? Time to look out for the WARNING SIGNS!

CHAPTER 5

Where there's SMOKE ...

The IRONY of BURNOUT is that often you don't KNOW you're burned out until you're in it, so it's important to take NOTICE of the SIGNS before things go TOO FAR.

To start with, the SIMPLEST thing you can do right now is take a GOOD, HONEST LOOK in the MIRROR!

There are TWO other ways to tell whether you're getting BURNED OUT.

The FIRST is to listen to what your BODY is telling you through the following SIGNS and SYMPTOMS:

EXHAUSTION

I'm WIPED OUT and I've just WOKEN UP!

Are you tired ALL the time?

That is NOT normal!

A clear sign of ADRENAL burnout is ongoing EXHAUSTION and FATIGUE. Most days, you can't find any ENERGY and feel completely SPENT – even if you haven't done a lot of physical activity.

CRAVINGS

When your body is STRESSED, you will tend to crave CAFFEINE, SUGAR and CARBS.

This is your body's way to COMPENSATE for feeling DEPLETED by seeking a quick ENERGY BOOST from these sources. While it helps for a short period of time, this 'hit' tends to be followed by a SLUMP, leaving you feeling even MORE exhausted!

BRAIN FOG

You're feeling CLUMSY and FORGETFUL. You're making silly MISTAKES, losing FOCUS and making POOR DECISIONS.

MEMORY LOSS, in particular, is a sure sign that your body is under a lot of STRESS.

Stress and constant 'BUSYNESS' impact the brain's EXECUTIVE FUNCTION, making it hard for your brain to function properly.

MORE FREQUENT ILLNESS

You can get SICK more often than before, with COLDS, FLU and a range of AUTOIMMUNE ailments.

Not only do you get sick MORE OFTEN, but it can also take LONGER for you to recover because your body's ability to FIGHT OFF and BOUNCE BACK from illness has been severely COMPROMISED. You may also notice NEW physical complaints manifesting and getting worse, including HEADACHES, MUSCULAR STIFFNESS, SKIN RASHES and DIGESTIVE PROBLEMS.

INSOMNIA

Even though you're EXHAUSTED, you simply can't get to SLEEP.

When you're constantly stressed, you remain on HIGH ALERT for potential DANGER or THREAT (real or imagined), and your body responds in KIND and struggles to SWITCH OFF.

Think of it in terms of an OVER-REVVED engine. The FASTER the engine is RUNNING, the longer it takes for it to SLOW DOWN.

Alternatively, you may PASS OUT from sheer exhaustion as soon as you hit the pillow, only to wake in the EARLY HOURS and be unable to go back to sleep.

WEIGHT GAIN

You may notice that you have put on WEIGHT almost without TRYING, especially around your BELLY.

Stress wreaks HAVOC on your METABOLISM by stimulating high levels of CORTISOL (the primary STRESS HORMONE produced by the adrenal glands). This can lead to INCREASED APPETITE and drives CRAVINGS, making it easier for you to accumulate BELLY FAT.

WEIGHT LOSS

Conversely, you may be losing KILOS at a similar rate without really TRYING!

If you are BURNED OUT, your body is working OVERTIME. Because stress continuously stimulates your MUSCLES to be ready for ACTION, this can deplete your supplies of GLYCOGEN (a derivative of glucose that's a form of energy storage). Being constantly 'pumped' eats away at your energy reserves, causing you to LOSE WEIGHT.

FLATLINE LIBIDO

You may just not feel like having SEX, and you're so TIRED and WIRED, you'd happily trade it for SLEEP!

Even at the best of times, LIBIDO is a delicate dance among several factors – PHYSICAL, MENTAL, EMOTIONAL and HORMONAL. If you are severely STRESSED, it is not surprising that your sex drive may take a NOSEDIVE.

Conversely, your sex drive may actually SPIKE. This may be driven by a desire for COMFORT or DISTRACTION.

Either way, it's not the USUAL!

Along with the above, there are numerous SIGNS of excess TENSION in the body. These may include:

- HEADACHES/MIGRAINES
- FLU-LIKE SYMPTOMS (without having the flu)
- TINNITUS (ringing sounds in the ears)
- BLURRED VISION
- SKIN IRRITATIONS (such as eczema)
- NECK AND SHOULDER TIGHTNESS
- DIGESTIVE PROBLEMS

And you're likely to be doing MORE of these …

OVEREATING   **DRINKING**   **SMOKING**

… which, of course, only makes things WORSE. You could wind up in a VICIOUS CYCLE of feeling BAD but doing more of the things that make you feel WORSE …

… until finally, something has to GIVE to make you STOP.

The bottom line is – if you don't stop VOLUNTARILY, your BODY will probably MAKE you stop, through SERIOUS and potentially LETHAL illnesses such as HEART FAILURE and LIVER DYSFUNCTION.

Having covered the PHYSICAL signs of burnout, we now turn to how you may be affected on the EMOTIONAL and PSYCHOLOGICAL levels. Signs of BURNOUT in this arena may include:

EASILY IRRITATED

You feel TENSE and CRANKY, and the slightest thing can set you off into a RAGE.

Being in a constant state of AGITATION can cause heightened SENSITIVITY. More things will 'trigger' you that you once might have hardly noticed and you could more prone to ANGRY OUTBURSTS.

One indication is if you find that people are AVOIDING you or walking on EGGSHELLS around you.

LACKING MOTIVATION

Things you used to ENJOY may now leave you FLAT; you just can't raise any ENTHUSIASM for many aspects of your life.

Of course, if your energy is SAPPED, this also diminishes your ability to fully ENGAGE in life.

MOOD SWINGS

Your moods can become UNPREDICTABLE. You might feel reasonably okay one minute, then an EMOTIONAL wreck the next with little or no WARNING.

Again, this can be attributed to swings in your HORMONES caused by STRESS.

DEPRESSION

You feel LOW. From where you are, life looks BLEAK and you may begin to LOSE HOPE of it ever improving.

While BURNOUT does not AUTOMATICALLY result in CLINICAL DEPRESSION, it can certainly make you more vulnerable to becoming depressed if you are PREDISPOSED to it.

CRYING JAGS

You may find yourself in TEARS at the DROP OF A HAT, even in fairly BENIGN situations.

While CRYING has a reputation as a sign of WEAKNESS, your body actually KNOWS what it's DOING!

CRYING releases the pressure of all that STRESS and it has other benefits such as lowering BLOOD PRESSURE, releasing STRESS HORMONES and reducing MANGANESE – a mineral that affects MOOD and is associated with ANXIETY in high levels. But REGULAR or ERRATIC bouts of crying tell you ONE THING – you're under TOO MUCH pressure!

RELATIONSHIP STRAIN

You may find yourself more at ODDS with others. You can have trouble being SOCIABLE. You can feel CRANKY and FLAT.

Let's face it – if you're BURNED OUT, you're NOT exactly FUN to be around! Even though this isn't really your FAULT, the changes in your character can take a HEAVY TOLL on your relationships.

After all, how much sustained LOVE, TOLERANCE, PATIENCE and UNDERSTANDING can a friend or loved one OFFER?

> You sure are HIGH MAINTENANCE these days!

Over time, there is a RISK of the relationship COLLAPSING under the STRAIN.

PANIC ATTACKS/ANXIETY

> I feel TERRIFIED and I don't know WHY!

> What's HAPPENING to me?

You can't BREATHE, your heart is RACING and you have an overwhelming sense of DREAD – as if something HORRIBLE is going to happen.

As I have explored in great detail in my previous books, ANXIETY and PANIC ATTACKS can occur when you are in OVERDRIVE. Too much STRESS (and an inability to MANAGE it) can trigger an inner 'ALARM SYSTEM' in the body and you remain in FLIGHT OR FIGHT mode.

When this happens, your mind and body are in a state of HYPERVIGILANCE, in which you perceive THREAT or DANGER everywhere – even if there is none. This is when you remain on HIGH ALERT and your body and mind respond as a means of PROTECTING you.

FLIGHT OR FIGHT is a natural response when there is a PERCEIVED threat to our SURVIVAL. It is HARD-WIRED into us and dates back to prehistoric times.

In ancient times, we had to be ALERT to potential DANGERS such as:

PREDATORS   **ENEMIES**

SHORTAGE OF SURVIVAL NEEDS

PHYSICAL DANGERS

The same INSTINCTIVE response still occurs today when our sense of SECURITY is threatened – either PHYSICALLY or EMOTIONALLY.

The anxious nature of your THOUGHTS and your system being OVERLY STIMULATED can fuel ANXIETY relating to burnout. This can be EXACERBATED if you've relied on too many of the STIMULANTS mentioned earlier to keep going.

Reaching this point (or any of the ABOVE) is NOT fun!

Suddenly, everything you've been STRIVING for can be OVERRUN by the STRUGGLE you now face.

BURNOUT presents you with this question: 'Is whatever you're doing WORTH all THIS?'

CHAPTER 6

If you CAN'T take the HEAT ...

While you may have the best of INTENTIONS, your CHOSEN FIELD, VOCATION or willingness to HELP and SERVE humanity may actually be putting you in the FIRING LINE for burnout – especially if you have a SENSITIVE or EASILY STRESSED nature.

The following factors, which are common to HIGH-STRESS occupations, can put workers at GREATER RISK of burnout:

Experiencing CRITICISM or AGGRESSION in the workplace (such as HELPLINE or CUSTOMER SERVICE workers).

PRESSURE to be always 'on' and AVAILABLE after hours or on weekends, even if you're feeling UNWELL or in a time of PERSONAL CRISIS (such as EXECUTIVES or SPECIALISTS).

EXPECTATIONS placed upon you to get MORE DONE than is humanly POSSIBLE in a workday.

Being BULLIED, subjected to INAPPROPRIATE BEHAVIOURS or 'GASLIGHTED' in the workplace. (Although there are now more REGULATIONS to prevent this, you may still feel too INTIMIDATED or AFRAID of losing your job to complain.)

NOT being APPRECIATED or receiving SUPPORT for your CONTRIBUTION as a worker.

Being paid LOW WAGES for the AMOUNT of WORK involved in the job.

Lacking a WORK-LIFE balance. Your work commitments mean MISSING important personal MILESTONES and CONNECTIONS.

Not making PROGRESS in your career can leave you feeling UNAPPRECIATED and STAGNANT.

If there are not enough STAFF to do the work, your tasks may be EXTENDED well beyond your JOB DESCRIPTION.

Now, let's now take a look at the OCCUPATIONS most associated with BURNOUT.

DOCTOR/PHYSICIAN

BURNOUT RISK FACTORS:

- LIFE-OR-DEATH DECISIONS

- HEAVY EMOTIONAL TOLL

- LONG HOURS

- LITTLE SLEEP

Particularly during the recent experience of COVID-19, the general DEMANDS on HEALTH WORKERS have escalated to an almost INTOLERABLE level. More people in these fields (and others such as RETAIL

WORKERS) are thus more likely to succumb to BURNOUT than before.

Not ALL physicians experience burnout at the same rate, however. SPECIALISTS, such as cardiologists and oncologists, are less likely to burn out than EMERGENCY PHYSICIANS and GENERAL PRACTITIONERS.

(We'll explore why some people are LESS LIKELY to BURN OUT than others in CHAPTER 15: THE SECRET HERBS AND SPICES.)

NURSE

BURNOUT RISK FACTORS:

- LIFE-OR-DEATH DECISIONS

- HEAVY EMOTIONAL TOLL

- LONG HOURS

- LITTLE SLEEP

While NURSES are exposed to the same BURNOUT RISKS as DOCTORS, nurses are more likely to be on the FRONT LINE, dealing with people on a more INTIMATE level, who are physically and emotionally DISTRESSED and often FRIGHTENED.

Nurses can also often feel UNAPPRECIATED or OVERLOOKED, and they tend to be lower on the PECKING ORDER.

RETAIL, FAST-FOOD AND CUSTOMER SERVICE

BURNOUT RISK FACTORS:

- SUBJECT TO CRITICISM, BAD BEHAVIOUR AND/OR ABUSE

- LONG HOURS

- LOW PAY

There are also limited opportunities for PROMOTION, and attaining a MANAGEMENT position often means working a lot of OVERTIME.

SOCIAL WORK

BURNOUT RISK FACTORS:

- STRESSFUL WORKING ENVIRONMENTS

- SECONDARY TRAUMATIC DISTRESS

- HIGH CASELOADS

- OVERWORK

Research shows that SOCIAL WORKERS are likely to experience BURNOUT at LEAST once in their career, mainly due to working in often EMOTIONALLY DISTRESSING situations on a DAILY basis.

FIRST RESPONDER

BURNOUT RISK FACTORS:

- HIGH RISKS

- LONG HOURS

- DISTURBED SLEEP PATTERNS

- EXPOSURE TO HIGHLY DISTURBING SCENARIOS

Included in this group are POLICE, PARAMEDICS and AMBULANCE WORKERS, FIREFIGHTERS, RESCUE WORKERS and staff at EMERGENCY call centres. DOCTORS and NURSES can also be in this category.

For POLICE OFFICERS, BURNOUT can mainly arise from WITNESSING the worst of humanity, as well as facing potential INJURY or even DEATH in their job.

Other factors may include SUPPRESSING EMOTIONS and unhealthy COPING STRATEGIES (such as drinking) because of the profession's traditionally 'STOIC' nature, where emotions are often INTERNALISED.

TEACHER

BURNOUT RISK FACTORS:

- EXPOSURE TO DIFFICULT STUDENTS

- HEAVY AFTER-HOURS WORKLOAD

- LOW PAY

The PANDEMIC has shown many parents just how DIFFICULT a teacher's job is. Teachers not only have to deal with students who aren't always WELL BEHAVED, but also do a significant amount of work that happens AFTER HOURS: preparing lesson plans, grading, etc.

AGED-CARE WORKER

BURNOUT RISK FACTORS:

- PHYSICALLY DEMANDING

- EMOTIONALLY TAXING

- LOW PAY

There are many demands for people who work with OLDER PEOPLE, such as the DEATH of someone you may have formed an attachment to, and attending to people who may be CHRONICALLY ILL, LONELY or in various stages of DEMENTIA – some of whom may display AGGRESSIVE or highly DEMANDING behaviours. Typically, this field is also low paid.

Well, my career isn't on this LIST but I can tell you, it's EVERY BIT as demanding as those that ARE!

Any CAREER that involves the following can put you at risk of BURNOUT:

- CRITICAL DECISION-MAKING

- EXTENSIVE TRAVEL

- HAVING TO BE ON-CALL

- CARING FOR OTHERS

- HEAVY CASELOAD

- VARIABLE ROSTER

- DEALING WITH THE GENERAL PUBLIC (especially handling complaints or working on helplines)

- HIGH WORKLOAD and LOW WAGES

- EXCESSIVE RESPONSIBILITY

- EXCESSIVE OVERTIME

- HIGH INVESTMENT IN THE BUSINESS

Any career can lead to BURNOUT. But is it the CAREER or how you MANAGE it?

Not all workers on the above list fall prey to BURNOUT. Some COPE WELL with the DEMANDS of the job and can continue in their profession for many years WITHOUT SUCCUMBING to burnout.

If you are choosing your career path, however, it may be wise to make your ability to handle stress PHYSICALLY, MENTALLY and EMOTIONALLY a key factor when considering your PROFESSION.

CHAPTER 7

HOME-COOKED

Another role associated with BURNOUT is that of the CARER.

Through various CIRCUMSTANCES, you may find yourself being responsible for the CARE and WELFARE of someone who is UNWELL, INCAPACITATED, DISABLED or even DYING.

Today, there are many more SUPPORT SERVICES and RESOURCES available for carers than in the past, but it is important to remember that YOU are the one on the FRONT LINE.

While you may have taken on this role as an act of KINDNESS or LOVE, or out of a sense of DUTY, the risks to your own WELLBEING in taking on this role shouldn't be OVERLOOKED.

Caregiver burnout is a state of PHYSICAL, EMOTIONAL and MENTAL exhaustion, which may lead to the following:

YOU STOP CARING ...

You may START OUT with your heart in the RIGHT PLACE, but burnout can slowly ERODE your ATTITUDE.

BURNOUT can happen if you don't get the HELP you need, or if you try to do MORE than you're able, either PHYSICALLY or FINANCIALLY.

... OR YOU CARE TOO MUCH

Your entire life begins to REVOLVE AROUND attending to the NEEDS of the person in your care, while your OWN NEEDS take SECOND PLACE.

ROLE CONFUSION

You may feel CONFUSED in your new RELATIONSHIP as CARER to the person you are looking after.

It can be HARD to separate this role from that of SPOUSE, PARTNER, CHILD or FRIEND – possibly, this was someone you once TURNED TO in your own times of NEED.

PAINFUL EMOTIONS

You may be witnessing the DECLINE – or even DEMISE – of this person you LOVE.

This can be especially PAINFUL if the person in your care is sliding into DEMENTIA.

UNREALISTIC EXPECTATIONS

You may have OVERESTIMATED the IMPACT your care would have on the OUTCOME of the patient.

You may also have expected, but not received, ACKNOWLEDGEMENT or GRATITUDE for your sacrifices. And because of their feelings of HELPLESSNESS, the person you are looking after may actually RESENT being in your care.

TAKING ON THE SOLE BURDEN

You may feel you have had no CHOICE but to take on this role, and find that it is TOO MUCH for you, alone.

This may lead to RESENTMENT if you feel you have taken on all the RESPONSIBILITY while others have NEGLECTED theirs.

LACKING RESOURCES

You may have had to give up a HEALTHY INCOME to become a CARER, and you may struggle to MANAGE the many COSTS and PHYSICAL DEMANDS involved.

You may also feel you don't have the necessary RESOURCES and SKILLS to manage your loved one's care WELL ENOUGH.

TOO MANY SACRIFICES

The LIFESTYLE changes required to be a CARER are SIGNIFICANT. You may feel a SENSE of LOSS or even GRIEF for the life you once had.

You may miss things like a CAREER, SOCIAL OUTINGS, RELATIONSHIPS, HOBBIES and INTERESTS, TRAVEL and the ability to be SPONTANEOUS.

Here are some further SIGNS that you may be burned out as a CARER:

- Withdrawing from FRIENDS and FAMILY
- Feeling DOWN, IRRITABLE, HELPLESS and HOPELESS
- Changing APPETITE, WEIGHT or both
- Changing SLEEP PATTERNS
- Getting SICK more often

- Feeling EXHAUSTED emotionally and physically

- Overusing ALCOHOL and/or SLEEP and other MEDICATIONS

- Feeling like you want to HURT YOURSELF or even the PERSON in your care

Caregivers are often so busy caring for OTHERS that they tend to neglect themselves. You may not RECOGNISE when you're burned out and could get to the point where you can't FUNCTION. There is a danger of YOU becoming ill, too.

Unfortunately, CARER BURNOUT – just like other forms of burnout – can CREEP UP on you. At first, you think you can MANAGE, but the day-to-day reality may prove to be TOO MUCH.

NO – but have you explored all your OPTIONS BEFORE committing to this role? And if you are ALREADY committed, have you explored the RESOURCES available to you?

Here are some SUGGESTIONS:

- GET HELP – the SOONER the BETTER!

You may want to delay seeking help from a community support agency, but the sooner you REACH OUT, the better.

Especially in the case of a patient with DEMENTIA, the SOONER they can establish a familiar and trusted RELATIONSHIP with someone other than you, the FEWER the DEMANDS on you alone.

- Take regular BREAKS.

- Stay SOCIAL.

- Pay ATTENTION to your own NEEDS.

- Eat WELL.

- Get enough REST.

- Consider temporary RESPITE CARE
  and take a HOLIDAY.

- Join a SUPPORT GROUP.

A SPECIAL NOTE ON COMPASSION FATIGUE

Though not strictly categorised as BURNOUT and
not strictly confined to CARERS (COUNSELLORS,
PSYCHOLOGISTS and HEALTH WORKERS may also be
affected), too many demands on an otherwise CARING

and RESPONSIBLE person can result in a condition known as COMPASSION FATIGUE.

The signs of COMPASSION FATIGUE include:

- Feeling OVERWHELMED and DRAINED

- Feeling RESENTMENT towards the person in your care

- Not wanting to be AROUND the person and AVOIDING them (choosing to work late, daydreaming about no longer having to care for them, etc.)

- Having less PATIENCE and TOLERANCE

- Having out-of-character ANGRY OUTBURSTS

- Feeling CYNICAL and HOPELESS

- Impaired ability to make CARE DECISIONS

- Wanting to PHYSICALLY ATTACK the person (or actually doing this)

- DELIBERATELY IGNORING or NEGLECTING the person's CARE or NEEDS

All of the above are SIGNS that you've reached a point where the role has become TOO MUCH for you, and you need to seek HELP!

Well, I'm the PATIENT and I get BURNED OUT too!

Indeed, someone who has a CHRONIC ILLNESS or DISABILITY can also experience BURNOUT.

This may include people who are not necessarily confined to HOME or BEDRIDDEN, but who are trying to maintain a regular lifestyle and holding a job while living with an illness or disability.

The heavy TOLL of trying to live NORMALLY while experiencing considerable PAIN, CHRONIC FATIGUE or PHYSICAL DISCOMFORT can be EXHAUSTING. The DEMANDS on an already UNWELL person can be considerable and may include:

• FACING SOCIAL STIGMA

Particularly in Western culture, the quest for 'PERFECTION' is the holy grail, which is exacerbated by SOCIAL MEDIA. This can take a heavy toll on the SELF-ESTEEM of someone with an illness and/or disability.

• FEELING THE FINANCIAL DRAIN

The person with a disability may have many EXPENSES to help them maintain a regular lifestyle, including

MEDICATIONS and HEALTH CARE as well as TRANSPORT (including taxis, additional fares for carers and car modifications) and UTILITIES (including the extra costs of assistive technology). This means they can be less able to AFFORD the small LUXURIES that involve 'fitting in' with others.

• RELYING ON OTHERS

Having to RELY on others can be draining. This can result in feelings of HELPLESSNESS and a severe lack of SELF-CONFIDENCE. They can also lack PRIVACY.

• TRYING TO 'KEEP UP'

For people with a disability or illness, adopting the 'normal' routines of the WORKPLACE or on SOCIAL OUTINGS can involve COMPLEX procedures. They may need to accommodate many different factors to 'BELONG'.

• SICK OF BEING SICK

Feeling UNWELL or PHYSICALLY LIMITED at all times can lead to feeling 'FED UP'. Life may feel more like a BURDEN than a BLESSING.

All of the above can cause considerable STRESS on top of the original AILMENT, which can be the BREAKING POINT leading to BURNOUT.

CHAPTER 8

Out of the FRYING PAN ...

QUESTION: How do you turn BURNOUT into a GLOBAL PHENOMENON?

ANSWER: Have a PANDEMIC!

COVID-19 has put an even greater STRAIN on people already close to BURNOUT – and even those who weren't!

However, COVID BURNOUT has its own distinct characteristics. Let's look at the extensive list of UNIQUE CHALLENGES to living through the pandemic:

- BLURRED LINES between PROFESSIONAL and PERSONAL LIVES

- LONGER WORKING HOURS

- SOCIAL DISTANCING

- MORE SCREEN TIME

- LOCKDOWN STRESS

- FINANCIAL HARDSHIP

- UPENDED ROUTINES

- POLITICISING OF SAFETY MEASURES

- STRAIN OF SAFETY MEASURES

- INSECURITY ABOUT THE FUTURE

Let's look at these in detail:

- ## **WORK/HOME LIFE IMBALANCE**

Prior to the pandemic, our WORKDAYS and the HOURS we worked were broken up by GOING TO and FROM the workplace, taking regular BREAKS away from the desk and having a DESIGNATED workspace.

Now, all of these can blend into ONE.

The lack of the normal DEMARCATION between WORK and HOME (such as COMMUTING to the office or WALKING to a meeting), combined with MULTI-TASKING home duties along with work duties, means that we have no chance for the brain to RESET through these natural INTERVALS.

Bringing our WORK into our HOMES has many components that can add up to BURNOUT.

For a START, we are more likely to work LONGER hours because we are always AVAILABLE.

Parents may have to JUGGLE a range of DOMESTIC DEMANDS around their work COMMITMENTS, including HOME-SCHOOLING.

There is also the social factor of being away from WORK COLLEAGUES, whose physical PRESENCE can help to offset STRESS by offering ways to SHARE problems and ideas, and provide SOCIAL RELIEF.

- **SOCIAL DISTANCING PLUS MORE SCREEN TIME**

While the RATIONAL brain understands the need for SOCIAL DISTANCING and changing how we may INTERACT with others (such as video conferencing), the more PRIMITIVE and REACTIVE brain has TROUBLE accommodating the new rules.

Did you know that your BRAIN has certain RULES about what is the CORRECT distance from others, depending on your RELATIONSHIP with them?

PERSONAL SPACE is the region surrounding a person, which they regard as psychologically THEIRS. There is a certain DISTANCE that dictates the RELATIONSHIP we have with others, and changes to personal space can make us feel CONFUSED, ANGRY, INVADED or REJECTED. We can also MISTAKE the level of INTIMACY (or LACK thereof) we have with another person.

Before COVID-19, we pretty much managed to negotiate personal space INTUITIVELY, but the pandemic has turned this on its HEAD.

With VIDEO CALLS, faces are within 50 cm of us – the normal region of CLOSE or INTIMATE FRIENDS instead of SUPERIORS, COLLEAGUES or STRANGERS. As a result, we may be OVERLY FAMILIAR, not set appropriate BOUNDARIES, or feel INTIMIDATED and overly SCRUTINISED.

Conversely, social distancing rules have forced our LOVED ONES into a more DISTANT field, usually reserved for ACQUAINTANCES, which the brain may interpret as REJECTION.

The EMOTIONAL and COGNITIVE effort of managing these CONFLICTING MESSAGES can wear people down.

The actual FEAR of CLOSE PROXIMITY to others can add to our stress, which can cause CONFUSION about the best decision to make when it comes to SOCIAL situations.

MENTAL HEALTH   VS.   PHYSICAL HEALTH

On TOP of all this is the INVASION of SCREEN TIME in our lives.

While you may wish to KEEP UP with loved ones, if you've been on Zoom ALL DAY, you simply may not have it in you to make (or take) that VIDEO CALL.

SCREEN TIME is not limited to the WORKPLACE either. We may go from the PHONE to the COMPUTER to the TELEVISION without a break, all of which OVERLOADS the BRAIN and doesn't give it time to REST.

- **LOCKDOWN STRESS**

We either had TOO MUCH of each other or NOT ENOUGH of of others!

LOCKDOWNS during the pandemic took their TOLL on most people's MENTAL WELLBEING.

LOCKDOWN BURNOUT was common for people stuck at home for WEEKS or MONTHS on end. The enforced isolation was DISORIENTING for most people.

Those most likely to 'feel the burn' during lockdown were people who were ELDERLY or LONELY, juggling WORK and HOME duties, helping CHILDREN LEARN at home, facing FINANCIAL difficulties because of their WORKPLACE or BUSINESS being closed, ISOLATING from LOVED ONES, and living in UNHAPPY or even ABUSIVE relationships.

LOCKDOWN was especially wearing on those who did not like being ALONE or found it difficult to ENTERTAIN themselves, especially for more EXTRAVERTED people, because they often found it difficult to pass the time without their regular SOCIAL and RECREATIONAL pursuits.

Not being able to go OUTSIDE for longer than a minimum amount of time created a CLAUSTROPHOBIC feeling of being trapped, which could also take a toll on people's MENTAL HEALTH.

• FINANCIAL HARDSHIP

The sweeping CHANGES and RESTRICTIONS that the pandemic imposed meant that many people's WORK or BUSINESS was in jeopardy.

This was further compounded for PARENTS, who may have had to CHOOSE between their CAREER and staying HOME to care for or home-school their CHILDREN.

WOMEN tended to be the MOST affected by these changes, because they were more likely to opt to be the person TAKING OVER this role.

• UPENDED ROUTINES

The pandemic has taken a particular toll on CHILDREN, who have had their lives DISRUPTED by SCHOOL CLOSURES, a lack of SOCIAL CONTACT with FRIENDS and being forced to remain INDOORS during lockdowns.

In turn, this increased PARENTAL STRESS because many children showed signs of ANGER, FRUSTRATION, FEAR and GRIEF because of the major changes in their lives.

• ENFORCED SAFETY MEASURES

It didn't take long for the NOVELTY to wear off with the new RULES requiring people to wear MASKS, DISINFECT THEIR HANDS and AVOID CONTACT with others.

It also didn't take long for people to start 'POLICING' each other over these precautions, adding TENSION, ANGER and RESENTMENT to an already stressful time.

Not only did we start RESENTING the RULES, but we also started to resent their RESTRICTIVE nature.

We started to become burned out with COMPLYING and were more likely to FLAUNT the RULES.

Humans tend to only remain OBEDIENT for a certain amount of time and, owing to the INVISIBLE nature of the THREAT, many decided they were FED UP and would take their CHANCES, despite the fact that the danger was just as high as in the first days of COVID.

- **UNCERTAIN FUTURE**

I feel WORN OUT from not knowing what comes next (and fearing the worst!)

HUMANS are simply not good at handling UNCERTAINTY, and COVID-19 has brought uncertainty with it in BUCKETLOADS – especially about the FUTURE.

Not only this but also COVID has no known end date, which adds to feelings of HELPLESSNESS and OVERWHELM. Compounding this is the possibility of ILLNESS or even DEATH, striking almost at random.

Humans need to feel SECURE, and PROLONGED FEAR and CONCERN about the future can undermine your WELLBEING.

The HARD TRUTH is that COVID isn't going AWAY for a considerable amount of time.

It all feels so OVERWHELMING! No WONDER we're BURNED OUT!

Yes, it's UNDENIABLE that the pandemic has taken its TOLL but there are quite a few things you can do to OFFSET this – especially if you now WORK from HOME.

CLEARLY DEFINE WORKING HOURS – AND ANNOUNCE THEM!

LIMIT WORK CALLS AND EMAILS TO WORKING HOURS.

BE FULLY PRESENT TO AFTER-HOURS PLEASURES.

INDULGE IN THINGS YOU LIKE DOING.

MAKE YOUR RESTING BEHAVIOURS DIFFERENT FROM YOUR WORKING ONES.

TAKE MICROBREAKS ...

... AND SELF-CARE BREAKS.

DO AN ONLINE 'WATERCOOLER CHAT'.

REDUCE MEETING TIMES.

ISOLATE YOUR WORK SPACE.

On more of a BIG-PICTURE scale, instead of FRETTING about the future or LAMENTING the changes to life as you knew it, look for the GIFT in the PROBLEM.

When you look for MEANING in ADVERSITY, it can ENRICH your life.

Changing your OUTLOOK can mean the difference between GOING UNDER and BOUNCING BACK.

FINALLY, there are things you have CONTROL over and things you DON'T.

You may not have any control over WORLD EVENTS, but you do have ABSOLUTE CONTROL over how you RESPOND to them.

Does COVID-19 mean you have to run yourself into the GROUND just to keep going? Not at ALL!

PART 2

COOLING
down

CHAPTER 9

Too darn HOT

We've now explored the many COLOURS of BURNOUT, and you may find yourself anywhere on this SPECTRUM but it's never too late to TURN IT AROUND.

First, we need to take a look at the KEY INGREDIENT behind the ONSET of burnout:

STRESS

UNDERSTANDING how stress works is a great way to start to pull yourself OFF THE COALS!

The DETERMINING factor in whether or not you go over the edge is STRESS, but more ACCURATELY, it's how you HANDLE stress. Not all stress is the SAME and not all stress is BAD, as you will see.

Stress is a NORMAL human reaction and the human body is designed to EXPERIENCE and REACT to stress.

STRESS RESPONSES help your body to adjust and respond appropriately to STRESSORS such as new situations, challenges and dangers.

But it seems that EVERYONE is stressed these days!

What about in the OLD DAYS? Didn't everyone just GET ON WITH IT?

Perhaps the best way to answer that is to take a little HISTORY lesson.

STRESS, as we currently understand it regarding a PSYCHOLOGICAL state, is a relatively RECENT concept.

People were definitely STRESSED in the past, but the concept related more to being subjected to HARDSHIP, POVERTY or PHYSICAL AFFLICTION, rather than being a PSYCHOLOGICAL state.

I'm STRESSED!

Want to borrow my GOAT??

While it is difficult to QUANTIFY, the stress of MODERN TIMES may not EXCEED that of earlier times, but we are certainly subjected to a WIDER RANGE of STRESSORS than in the PAST. We are also more likely to IDENTIFY with being stressed than our PREDECESSORS.

In our current understanding of it, the term STRESS means a feeling of EMOTIONAL STRAIN and PRESSURE. It mainly arose during the intense period of INDUSTRIAL and SCIENTIFIC progress in the 18th and 19th centuries.

PHYSICAL SCIENCES – most notably engineering – began to use terms such as *stress, strain, resilience, pressure* and *elasticity* to describe TENSION within structures; however, these soon found their way into everyday language along with other terms such as *snapping/breaking point* to describe EMOTIONAL/PSYCHOLOGICAL states.

Unfortunately, the word STRESS tends to have mostly NEGATIVE connotations.

But it's BAD to be stressed, isn't it?

Not NECESSARILY.

There are DEGREES of stress as well as TYPES of stress – these will affect where you may find yourself on the journey to BURNOUT.

There is such a thing as GOOD STRESS! This is known as EUSTRESS (which has its roots in the word 'euphoria') and it can make you feel:

MOTIVATED

STIMULATED

I can DO it!

I'm PUMPED!

Of course, at the OTHER END of the scale is DISTRESS, which is when the pendulum has swung TOO FAR the OTHER WAY, as this diagram illustrates.

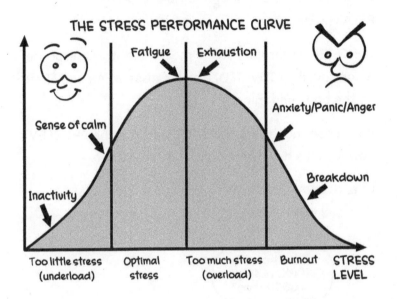

THE STRESS PERFORMANCE CURVE

Put simply, not ENOUGH stress and you're FLAT, BORED and UNPRODUCTIVE, while TOO MUCH stress leads to BURNOUT.

Like everything in life, there needs to be balance.

If you have TOO LITTLE stress, you can feel DRAINED, UNMOTIVATED and BORED. You need a BALANCE between EXTREMES to function well.

Stress can keep us ALERT, MOTIVATED and ready to RESPOND appropriately to HAZARDS. But stress becomes a PROBLEM when the stressors continue without RELIEF, or enough periods of REST or RELAXATION.

LONG-TERM (chronic) stress means the stress response is continually ACTIVATED, which causes WEAR and TEAR on the body and mind.

It is not so much that the STRESS itself is the PROBLEM, however, it's how the stress is MANAGED.

One GUARANTEED WAY to keep yourself STRESSED (in a bad way) is to be BUSY!

Sure – but are you being PRODUCTIVE?

Have you been saying THIS a lot lately?

Being BUSY can be seen as a BADGE of HONOUR. It can give you the APPEARANCE of being someone in HIGH DEMAND with unique SKILLS or ABILITIES that you, and only you, can bring to the situation, and for which you should be ADMIRED.

But is your 'BUSYNESS' getting you SOMEWHERE, or are you simply spinning your wheels in FRANTIC ACTIVITY under the ILLUSION that being BUSY will automatically get you there?

Being BUSY doesn't necessarily mean you are PRODUCTIVE.

Let's take a look.

BUSY	PRODUCTIVE
CREATES EXTRA AND UNNECESSARY TASKS	**GETS STRAIGHT ONTO MAIN TASK**

OVERESTIMATES WHAT CAN BE DONE

WORKS WITHIN ACHIEVABLE LIMITS

DOES EVERYTHING EXCEPT WHAT'S REQUIRED

STICKS TO THE PLAN

GETS DISTRACTED

STAYS FOCUSED

SAYS 'YES'
TOO QUICKLY

THINKS IT OVER
BEFORE AGREEING

NEVER HAS ENOUGH TIME

USES TIME EFFICIENTLY

TRIES TO BE PERFECT AT EVERYTHING

WORKS WITH WHAT'S AVAILABLE

What does it mean to be BUSY? Simply that you THINK you have a lot TO DO. But it doesn't actually mean you do what NEEDS to be DONE!

BUSYNESS means CRAMMING IN as much as you can. The problem is, once you get used to doing things in this way, it can become NORMAL to be frantic ALL the time!

In reality, you're not achieving much more than creating UNNECESSARY STRESS.

There are people who are in situations that are HIGH RISK or HIGH DEMAND, where part of being in that situation is to be subjected to MANY STRESSORS. But not everyone in those situations will end up with BURNOUT. We will explore WHY that is in the following chapters.

CHAPTER 10

The DISH or the COOK?

Here's a RECIPE for BURNOUT: take a handful of STRESSORS, mix in a PERSONALITY that's PRONE to STRESS and VOILA!

Commonly, people think that a SITUATION causes STRESS but the real issue is actually how you RESPOND to the situation.

Some people may even BLAME the BURNOUT for how they feel!

So, HOW did he GET so tired?

BURNOUT is the RESULT, not the CAUSE!

Let's look at two people with different outlooks facing a HIGH-PRESSURE situation. Who will CAVE IN first?

PERSON 1

PERSON 2

If you guessed PERSON 2 as the CANDIDATE to CRUMBLE, you're probably RIGHT!

Not only do we have a POTENTIALLY (but not NECESSARILY) stressful SCENARIO, we also have someone bringing HIGH and possibly UNREALISTIC expectations and demands into the mix, which GUARANTEES that the situation will be stressful!

PERSON 2 is most likely a 'TYPE A' personality, which is defined as DRIVEN, RESTLESS, tending to PERFECTIONISM, easily IRRITATED and HIGH ACHIEVING.

Interestingly, TYPE As are more likely to experience ANXIETY. Below are some of the TYPE A characteristics. Could these be part of the PROBLEM for you?

 Type As are always 'ON THE CLOCK' and always have SOMETHING TO DO.

Anything that SLOWS them down and keeps them from getting things done can feel like TORTURE.

Type As tend to have a GOAL-ORIENTED mindset and an intense drive to SUCCEED, and feel COMPELLED to KEEP GOING until that goal is achieved. They hate 'UNFINISHED BUSINESS'.

Type As are more prone to nervous behaviours, such as FIDGETING, NAIL-BITING and TEETH-GRINDING.

Type As don't have SPARE TIME– if they do, they FILL it! There NEVER seems to be ENOUGH TIME to do what they want. Time can have a feeling of URGENCY about it.

Type As tend to dwell on FRUSTRATIONS, WORRIES and REHASHES of unsettling experiences – especially when they lie down to SLEEP.

Haven't you got an INSTANT ENLIGHTENMENT program?

For Type As, taking valuable TIME OFF to RELAX can feel UNNATURAL and even STRESSFUL (because it wastes work time!) – unless relaxation itself is turned into a JOB!

Well, I've finished my LIFE'S WORK – now I'd better start ANOTHER!

You'd think that having COMPLETED a TO-DO LIST, it would be time to KICK BACK and enjoy the sense of ACHIEVEMENT but NO ... the Type A may just start a NEW ONE!

It doesn't take MUCH to set you OFF – you're so WIRED that your nerves are constantly on EDGE.

You're in COMPETITION with everyone and everything – including your WORKMATES, FRIENDS, NEIGHBOURS, FAMILY, the CLOCK, the CALENDAR and even YOURSELF!

Living this way is to be ADDICTED to STRESS, STRAIN and STRUGGLE.

CHAPTER 11

REVISING
the MENU

Not NECESSARILY.
Your PERSONALITY
develops as a
combination of
GENES and
ENVIRONMENT.

Your GENES do not DOOM you to live in an UNHEALTHY way! You are still free to CHOOSE how you live!

While many personality traits are INNATE, research suggests that Type A characteristics are more of a reaction to ENVIRONMENTAL FACTORS and can be influenced by how someone RESPONDS to stressful situations.

Yes! Which means you can MODIFY it.

Let's look at an example: baking a cake is a FORMULA, in which you have SPECIFIC INGREDIENTS (NATURE).

These are then subjected to any number of VARIABLES in how the cake is PREPARED and BAKED (NURTURE).

Same RECIPE – different CAKE!

This shows how ENVIRONMENT plays a significant role in INFLUENCING and MODIFYING behaviour.

The interplay between a person's INHERITED TEMPERAMENT (which defines how they THINK) and their ENVIRONMENT constantly RESHAPES their personality.

You may not generally be of an INTENSE, DRIVEN or WORKAHOLIC nature, but find yourself in a HIGH-PRESSURE, results/performance-driven, do-or-die environment or situation. In which case, it may be SINK or SWIM, and you will need to MODIFY your behaviour to accommodate the DEMANDS placed upon you.

No matter whether you are a Type A personality by NATURE, or whether you have arrived at BEHAVING like a Type A because of CIRCUMSTANCES, you may need to make some BIG CHANGES!

Let's take a moment to do an INVENTORY of what is BEHIND a Type A person's DRIVEN and EXHAUSTING approach to life, and how this might apply to YOU.

GOOD GRIEF!
I haven't got TIME for NAVEL-GAZING!

Think of it as an ESSENTIAL TASK, okay?

Would you rather be gazing at the ceiling of a HOSPITAL WARD instead?

So, as HONESTLY as you can – answer the FOLLOWING:

1. TODAY, how much time did you allocate to:

- WORK

- HOUSEWORK

- COMMUTING

- SHOPPING FOR ESSENTIALS

- SHOPPING FOR PLEASURE

- HOME MAINTENANCE

- PARENTING

- SOCIALISING

- EATING

- LEISURE ACTIVITIES

- EXERCISE

- SCREEN TIME (PHONE/COMPUTER/TELEVISION)

- QUIET REFLECTION

- RELAXATION

- QUALITY TIME WITH PARTNER/FAMILY

- SELF-CARE/GROOMING

- SLEEP?

2. Currently, how BALANCED would you say your life is in terms of EQUAL parts WORK, REST and PLAY?

3. How HAPPY are you generally?

4. Would you say your level of HAPPINESS has DECREASED?

5. Do you believe you will be HAPPIER in the FUTURE if you keep doing what you're doing?

6. Do you DELEGATE enough or do you do EVERYTHING yourself?

7. Why is that the CASE?

8. Do you TRUST others to do things as well as YOU can?

9. Do you loathe ASKING for HELP? If so, WHY?

10. What do you hope to ACHIEVE from all your current EFFORTS?

11. How will you know you have ACHIEVED your END GOAL?

12. Does your END GOAL include finding more PEACE, SATISFACTION and ENJOYMENT than you currently experience?

13. When will you allocate TIME for these things?

14. Can you settle for GOOD ENOUGH rather than PERFECT?

15. What do you think is DRIVING your need for PERFECTION?

16. Are you afraid of being judged a FAILURE if you GIVE UP this situation? Who will be doing the JUDGING? You or others?

17. Do you see driving yourself to the LIMIT as a BADGE OF HONOUR?

18. What do you FEAR will happen if you just STOP EVERYTHING?

19. How REALISTIC are these FEARS?

20. Why do you feel there's NEVER ENOUGH time?

21. Do you know what it means to JUST BE? Do you know HOW to 'just BE'?

Type A traits tend to run in OPPOSITION to many effective stress-management techniques, such as MEDITATION.

Given the Type A characteristics of IMPATIENCE, COMPETITIVENESS and frustration at WASTING TIME, sitting quietly and doing 'nothing' can feel like a form of TORTURE for the INTENSE Type A nature.

But all is not LOST! While it would be IDEAL if you could SOFTEN some aspects of being Type A, you can't and don't need to change your NATURE to manage stress in a HEALTHIER way, even within the parameters of your personality.

Here are some STRESS-MANAGEMENT TECHNIQUES that are specially tailored for Type As, but can also be helpful to other personality types.

NOT EVERYTHING IS A PROJECT!

Do you find that, even if you're doing a PLEASANT and RELAXING activity, your mind is still in WORK MODE?

Bring your ATTENTION to this and SWITCH OFF from WORK by reminding yourself to just DO what you're DOING – and NOTHING more!

Let's explore the EXAMPLE of going for a walk.
If you MUST make it an ASSIGNMENT, here are your INSTRUCTIONS:

- Look at the TREES. Notice how the leaves MOVE.

- Feel the BREEZE on your face. What does it FEEL like?

- Notice the SOUND of your feet on the footpath.

- What can you SMELL?

- Can you TASTE anything right now?

OVERDO IT!

I REALLY don't want to DO this but I HAVE to!

As CRAZY as it might seem, DELIBERATELY pushing yourself to an EXTREME (as opposed to FINDING yourself going to extremes) – particularly when you DON'T FEEL like it – can help you REALISE how FAR you PUSH yourself and could help you to BACK OFF.

Put in an ALL-NIGHTER when you're already TIRED or deliberately stand in a LONG QUEUE, just to show yourself that you CAN tolerate this.

FAKE IT TILL YOU MAKE IT

I'm going to PRETEND to be a really LAID-BACK person today!

Sometimes you can ACT your way into new ways of BEING. Have you ever really given being more LAID-BACK a SHOT?

By CONSCIOUSLY choosing to SLOW DOWN more often, you can START to incorporate a QUIETER PACE into your everyday life.

RECORD YOUR 'A' MOMENTS

Keep a daily RECORD of times you feel ANGRY, FRUSTRATED, IMPATIENT or OVERWHELMED. This can highlight PATTERNS and TRIGGERS that keep you in an intense LOOP.

GET PHYSICAL

All that TENSION needs an OUTLET, and no-one can benefit more from a TOUGH WORKOUT than a Type A! Try some form of EXERCISE that helps you RELEASE tension, such as BOXING or MARTIAL ARTS.

SETTLE FOR 'GOOD ENOUGH'

I can't do BETTER than my BEST!

Do you REALLY have to get it ALL done today?

Does it REALLY have to be PERFECT?

Can you find FULFILMENT in the DOING, rather than the ACHIEVING?

Can you EASE BACK enough to actually ENJOY what you're DOING?

OWN YOUR ANGER

GRRR!

Be HONEST now – you've got a lot of ANGER going on, don't you?

But WHO or WHAT are you actually angry with?

Writing down your feelings – especially your FRUSTRATIONS – can be a way of UNDERSTANDING what is really going on UNDERNEATH for you.

Working with a THERAPIST can be highly beneficial in helping you move through OLD HURTS that may be feeding your ANGER.

Finally, work at being a 'NICER' person. LISTEN more. SMILE more. ENGAGE with others, rather than COMPETING with or trying to OUTDO them. Instead of seeing 'ENEMIES' or 'RIVALS', look for potential FRIENDS and ALLIES.

CHAPTER 12

FEAR and the FLAMBÉ

There may be several PRACTICAL factors at play beyond PERSONALITY type that can cause someone to take on TOO MUCH, such as:

- You have FINANCIAL DEMANDS.

- Your JOB is on the LINE.

- You feel OBLIGATED or DUTY-BOUND.

- Your SITUATION involves a HIGH level of PRESSURE.

In these cases, you need to make PRACTICAL DECISIONS about whether or not you CONTINUE to PERSEVERE or MOVE ON.

However, there are OTHER factors that may lead someone to take on (and ENDURE) an unacceptably HIGH-PRESSURE situation, which may be less easily addressed, such as:

- LOW SELF-ESTEEM

- BEING OVERLY ACCOMMODATING

- NO CLEAR BOUNDARIES

- INFLATED SENSE OF RESPONSIBILITY

- RELUCTANCE/INABILITY TO SAY 'NO'

- FEAR OF 'LETTING OTHERS DOWN'

While these are examples of why someone might push past all reasonable limits, and put their health and wellbeing in JEOPARDY, there is usually one COMMON FACTOR behind this:

FEAR

Let's look at how fear is a DRIVING FORCE towards BURNING OUT.

FEAR OF NOT HAVING/NOT BEING ENOUGH

I CAN'T lose this job! I have to do WHATEVER IT TAKES!

This may appear to be an OBVIOUS reason to OVEREXTEND yourself – especially given the PRECARIOUS and COMPETITIVE aspects of holding on to a job in the current climate.

While PRACTICAL CONCERNS may be behind your decision to push yourself, the fear of NOT HAVING/ NOT BEING ENOUGH will probably be running you into BURNOUT, rather than helping you earn enough to ensure your SURVIVAL.

If you're driven to excess in the workplace, you may think there will never be enough TIME, MONEY, SECURITY, POSSESSIONS or COMFORTS. You may always believe you need MORE.

There can also be more SUBTLE fears driving you to BURNOUT, such as:

FEAR OF BEING OVERLOOKED

Again, this may arise if you are in a workplace environment where there is strong COMPETITION for key roles, but can also apply if you wish to EXCEL in personal or creative endeavours. It is driven by a desire to be SEEN and HEARD.

FEAR OF SPEAKING UP

If you are UNSURE of yourself or see other people as being more POWERFUL, you may have trouble ASSERTING yourself, even when subjected to UNREASONABLE DEMANDS.

FEAR OF CONFLICT

If you fear CONFLICT, you might go to ENORMOUS LENGTHS to avoid it.

This might mean AGREEING to things you don't wish to do.

FEAR OF DISAPPOINTMENT IN YOURSELF

This fear may arise when you STRIVE for impossibly HIGH STANDARDS and tend towards PERFECTIONISM.

FEAR OF LETTING OTHERS DOWN

This fear can lead to an exaggerated sense of 'DUTY' where you feel you have no CHOICE but to take on RESPONSIBILITY for 'FIXING' the situation.

However, what is driving this fear is often a 'NEED TO BE NEEDED'.

FEAR OF JUDGMENT/CRITICISM

You may be driving yourself out of a fear of being seen as a 'MALINGERER' or someone who is NOT UP to the TASK. You may be constantly COMPARING yourself to others and finding yourself LACKING.

FEAR OF FAILURE

This fear is common if you're someone who sees SUCCESS as the ULTIMATE GOAL in life.

Underlying this, of course, is a GREATER fear of being judged a failure by OTHERS.

FEAR OF FEELING GUILTY

You may feel OBLIGED to take on a particular responsibility, such as being a CARER for a relative or loved one.

You may feel like you have no CHOICE or SAY in it, or like you will be a 'BAD' person if you don't CARRY this through.

Have you noticed how many of these fears are fuelled by what OTHERS might THINK of you?

Often, people are pushing themselves to the limit to 'PROVE' something ...

... either to THEMSELVES ...

... or to OTHERS, as an act of DEFIANCE.

Either way, you may be running on a FEAR of being deemed UNWORTHY and feeling you have to PROVE OTHERWISE.

But why would people try to prove their WORTH by MISTREATING themselves?

We are very much moulded by EARLY MESSAGES about our WORTH and CAPABILITIES, and by the EXPECTATIONS placed upon us by others – especially those who play INFLUENTIAL roles in our UPBRINGING.

These CHILDHOOD messages have a strong IMPACT on how we PERCEIVE ourselves and automatically play out well into ADULTHOOD.

Messages that may drive someone to PUSH themselves beyond reasonable limits may include:

CRITICISM

FAMILY VALUES

DREAMS BEING QUASHED

HIGH EXPECTATIONS

The desire for ACCEPTANCE and APPROVAL (or, more accurately, the desire to avoid REJECTION and DISAPPROVAL) can even override SELF-PRESERVATION and cause someone to push well beyond their limits.

But there is one more, even GREATER fear that keeps someone in this dynamic. We'll look at that NEXT.

CHAPTER 13

Another LOG on the FIRE

So now we come to the MAIN fear driving you to BURN OUT — even when you realise you can't GO ON like this:

FEAR OF STOPPING

You KNOW where PUSHING yourself is heading. You KNOW it's HURTING you but you can't — or, more accurately, WON'T — stop.

In this sense, driving yourself is as much an ADDICTION as any other STIMULANT.

And an ADDICTION to anything is a desire to ESCAPE from experiencing the inner EMPTINESS that the addictive element is used to keep at bay.

To ANSWER that question, all you need to do is STOP and see what COMES UP.

What does it FEEL like to STOP? What does it feel like when you CEASE the constant ACTIVITY?

When you STOP, you're left with YOURSELF. And let's FACE IT, you've been TOO BUSY to be with yourself for a LONG TIME, haven't you?

When you STOP, you come face to face with the REAL ISSUE – the DISCOMFORT of being with YOURSELF.

Ultimately, it's not the JOB, OBLIGATION or DUTY that is causing you to keep PUSHING – it's the fear of the VACUUM that stopping brings with it.

Instead of filling the VACUUM with more work or FEVERISH ACTIVITY, pause for a moment and consider what might fill that space INSTEAD.

What are you actually SEEKING by striving until you BURN OUT?

Have you ASKED for that, or do you just HOPE it will happen?

I want someone to RECOGNISE how HARD it is for ME!

Someone could POSSIBLY take PITY on you and STEP IN, but what if they DON'T? If you're LOOKING for a SAVIOUR before you stop, you're setting yourself up for DISAPPOINTMENT.

The ONLY person who can SAVE you is YOU.

So, what do you want MORE OF, but do not ALLOW yourself to HAVE?

It might be:

- REST

- PLAY

- SPACE

- SOMEONE TO LISTEN

- A MORE RELAXED LIFESTYLE

- PEOPLE TO SHARE THE LOAD

- RECOGNITION FOR YOUR EFFORTS

- HELP TO STOP DOING THIS

Was there a time when this was WORKING for you before it tipped into BURNOUT?

What was happening when it WORKED WELL?

Can you remember what CHANGED to turn this from a PLEASURE into a BURDEN?

The BOTTOM LINE IS:

- What do you need to stop RUNNING FROM?

- What do you need to EMBRACE MORE OF?

CHAPTER 14

Here's one I PREPARED earlier

There is one fear that we haven't covered in the previous chapters:

FEAR OF THE FUTURE

I have to PREVENT the WORST!

COVID-19 has certainly brought this fear to the FOREFRONT, reinforced by fears of CLIMATE CHANGE and the threat of GLOBAL CONFLICT.

People may push themselves in the PRESENT to 'INSURE' themselves against an uncertain FUTURE.

It is important to note here that, despite CURRENT and highly VISIBLE concerns about the FUTURE, this is NOT a NEW TREND.

People have ALWAYS pushed themselves to SHORE UP their future! Why ELSE would you do it?

While it is SENSIBLE to *make hay while the sun shines* to ensure your SURVIVAL, there is a vast difference between gathering what you NEED in the PRESENT and working yourself to DEATH for a FUTURE that, if you keep going at this rate, you MIGHT NOT get to SEE!

In fact, there IS no tomorrow!

Tomorrow is a MYTH, because it hasn't HAPPENED yet!

And an even GREATER myth, perpetuated by

FAIRYTALES ...

**... TV SHOWS, BOOKS,
SONGS, MOVIES ...**

... AND ADVERTISING ...

… has us HYPNOTISED into thinking that TOMORROW will be BETTER than TODAY or YESTERDAY.

The truth is, there's no GUARANTEE that the FUTURE is going to be ANYTHING other than what it TURNS OUT to be, simply because it DOESN'T EXIST!

Think of it THIS way … According to the human construct we call 'TIME', you leave YESTERDAY and enter TOMORROW at the stroke of midnight, but are things any DIFFERENT from a SECOND ago?

There is only NOW and NOW and NOW – a series of NOWS that become our version of 'REALITY'.

You're therefore creating your FUTURE, right now, in the PRESENT.

We can be holding out for MIRACLES, INTERVENTIONS and LUCK, hoping for a better TOMORROW that we're convinced is waiting for us. Meanwhile, we can be SQUANDERING all that we have RIGHT NOW!

There is NEVER going to be a magical CHANGE for the BETTER in the FUTURE unless you make that change in the PRESENT.

That means if you are UNHAPPY with your situation, you need to make changes for the better NOW, otherwise your situation will stay the SAME.

The harsh truth is that we never know when our lives may END, or when TRAGEDY, ACCIDENT or NATURAL DISASTER may occur. The PANDEMIC has shown

how everything can change in the BLINK of an EYE.
Suddenly, all the things we'd PLANNED for TOMORROW
weren't even an OPTION anymore. You simply cannot
shore up enough to cover ALL CONTINGENCIES.

But – who KNOWS? There is an equal CHANCE that
your life might go SWIMMINGLY!

And the PRESENT includes (or should include) ALL the things you've been DENYING yourself.

Living in the PRESENT frees you to:

- FOLLOW YOUR HEART

- BE SPONTANEOUS

- TAKE SOME RISKS

- HAVE FUN

- RELEASE UNNECESSARY BURDENS

- LIVE THE LIFE YOU *WANT* TO LIVE

Living in the PRESENT can release you from the PULL of the PAST and the PUSH to mould a FUTURE that is going to do its own thing anyway!

When you EMBRACE the truth that all you have is NOW, you have the OPTION to make the BEST of it.

CHAPTER 15

The SECRET herbs and spices

Some people actually THRIVE in high-stress and demanding roles, and don't succumb to BURNOUT!

While it's clear that 'BAD' stress often leads to burnout, it's important to note that STRESS and BURNOUT are not the SAME thing.

It is entirely possible to handle situations that may be experienced as 'HIGH STRESS' – including LONG HOURS, HEAVY RESPONSIBILITIES and HIGH INTENSITY – without falling into the emotional EXHAUSTION, DISENCHANTMENT and total DEPLETION that come with BURNOUT.

Actually, that's TRUE. My friend is in a very HIGH-STRESS job and he seems to ENJOY it!

YES! Not every CEO, first responder, carer or teacher (for example) becomes BURNED OUT (we'd be in real TROUBLE if they did!), so clearly it is not just the SITUATION that causes BURNOUT.

We have explored some of the PERSONALITY factors that help set up people to develop BURNOUT in our exploration of the TYPE A response to life, but there are other INGREDIENTS that can help people avoid becoming burned out – regardless of the STRESS involved in their situation.

People who don't get burned out know how to do the FOLLOWING:

DETACH   **DEBRIEF**

DELIBERATE

DECOMPRESS

This is known as EMOTIONAL INTELLIGENCE.

EMOTIONAL INTELLIGENCE (also known as Emotional Quotient or EQ) is the ability to UNDERSTAND, USE and MANAGE your emotions in positive ways to RELIEVE stress, COMMUNICATE effectively, EMPATHISE with others, OVERCOME challenges and DEFUSE conflict.

Let's take a look at when the MAGIC INGREDIENT of
EMOTIONAL INTELLIGENCE is APPLIED, versus when
it is NOT:

CONFLICT MANAGEMENT   **LACK OF**

A person with high EMOTIONAL INTELLIGENCE can manage even EXTREMELY STRESSFUL situations by MAINTAINING their EQUILIBRIUM and PROTECTING their own WELLBEING.

There are several TECHNIQUES you can learn to help you respond more EFFECTIVELY in STRESSFUL situations by applying EMOTIONAL INTELLIGENCE:

- **STOP FEEDING YOUR STRESS**
  Too often, we're actually the SOURCE of our own stress. We can do this with how we THINK about the situation. We can often CREATE stress in our MINDS even before anything OCCURS.

- **PACE YOURSELF**
  EVERYONE has a LIMIT! RECOGNISE yours and PULL BACK before you REACH it. Ask for HELP if you need it.

- **GET OUT OF 'DEFENCE MODE'**
  Remember, NOBODY is 'out to get you'. The WORLD is not your ENEMY. You don't need to be constantly ON GUARD or PUSHING yourself to the LIMIT.

- **BE POSITIVE**
  Try seeing things in a different LIGHT and from a more OPTIMISTIC perspective. This means changing your PERSPECTIVE on how you VIEW your situation. It's only as bad (or good) as you THINK it is!

So, we now look at the second MAGIC INGREDIENT – LOVE.

If you LOVE what you do, if it gives you a THRILL, if you get SATISFACTION from doing what you do, if instead of STRESS you feel ENERGISED, then, quite simply, you're unlikely to get BURNED OUT!

It's not the LONG HOURS, CHALLENGES or COMPLEXITIES of a situation that can cause you to feel BURNED OUT – it is the RESISTANCE you feel towards these things.

Test this out for YOURSELF. When you are FULLY ENGAGED and ENJOYING YOURSELF, you can go well beyond what you think are your LIMITS. Notice when it starts to TIP from PLEASURE into PAIN – that's when to take a BREAK, STOP for now or GIVE IT UP completely!

Start LOVING what you do, loving YOURSELF and loving LIFE more, and see what happens!

The THIRD magic ingredient is your INNER CHILD. How long has it been since you've PLAYED, LAUGHED or felt WONDER?

Your inner child NEEDS those things!

Your INNER CHILD can also alert you to your ADULT NEEDS! Too often, we OVERRIDE our basic needs such as HUNGER, REST, RELAXATION or even TOILET BREAKS to finish that REPORT or run that ERRAND!

When a child is HUNGRY, they need to eat, NOW! When a child is TIRED, they need to rest, NOW! When you learn to IMMEDIATELY respond to your human needs, you are giving YOURSELF (and, by proxy, your inner child) the ATTENTION and CARE you DESERVE.

The FINAL magic ingredient is HOME.

People who go home to SECURITY, SAFETY, SUPPORT and SANCTUARY are less likely to DRIVE themselves into the GROUND.

But I'm ALL ALONE! How can I find those things?

'HOME' does not necessarily mean FAMILY in the CONVENTIONAL sense.

'HOME' can be anywhere you feel that you can REST and be at PEACE, and where you are surrounded by the things that make you feel SECURE and GROUNDED.

'HOME' can be your COMMUNITY, your FRIENDS, your PETS, your TREASURES, your favourite MUSIC, your HOBBIES or your best RECIPE.

If you do not have a sense of 'HOME' that is as IMPORTANT in your life as your ENDEAVOURS, then creating a sense of 'HOME' absolutely needs to be your NEXT STEP!

CHAPTER 16

DOUSING the FLAME

You know you need to STOP this, don't you?

For WHAT?

Let's get this STRAIGHT –
nobody is going to
RESCUE you or successfully
INTERVENE until YOU
decide to CHANGE the
way you do life.

Let's not KID OURSELVES –
changing how you behave
is not EASY but it IS doable!

And the BEST WAY to start is by STARTING. By making
SMALL changes, you can begin to see that there is
ANOTHER WAY, which feels a whole lot BETTER!

If you need some help – ASK for it! This might mean recruiting a LIFE COACH or COUNSELLOR to help you break some old, entrenched PATTERNS and address the FEARS that keep you STALLED.

Yes, there's always the possibility that you could end up POORER but RICHER!

It means choosing PEACE of MIND over PROSPERITY or POSSESSIONS.

You may be poorer in a MATERIAL sense, but far richer in terms of your HEALTH and WELLBEING.

Making that sort of change is RISKY! I might find myself STRUGGLING to make ends meet!

As we have explored, there are NO GUARANTEES of 'happy ever after' in ANY situation, so why not FOLLOW YOUR HEART?

Of course, it may be too STRESSFUL to leave your job but there are still things you can do to IMPROVE how you WORK.

What if you set the INTENTION, *'I want to feel inspired and challenged every day'*? How might this convert STRESS into PASSION?

If your job has been stressful enough to affect your HEALTH, talk to your BOSS and ask for HELP in reviewing the EXPECTATIONS placed upon you against your ability to MEET them. ASK them for what you NEED to ease the LOAD.

Okay, so NOW is the time to LET GO. Are you READY?

Well, I know I can't GO ON like this!

THAT'S all you need to know to get STARTED.

Here are a few final TIPS to help you MOVE ON:

- **GET SOCIAL AND STAY SOCIAL**

The saying 'All work and no play makes Jack a dull boy' has some WISDOM in it (even though, unfortunately, it's not gender-neutral). Let's face it: a DRUDGE isn't much fun to be around! HANGING OUT and LETTING LOOSE with others can have numerous benefits, such as a sense of BELONGING, increased SELF-ESTEEM, more RELAXATION and a greater sense of SECURITY.

- ## MAKE YOUR OWN WELLBEING THE PRIORITY TASK

Make being your BEST SELF the goal! Your best self is NOT this DRIVEN, EXHAUSTED, OVER-STRETCHED being! Your best self is WELL-RESTED, has plenty of ENERGY, is ENTHUSIASTIC, easily MANAGES tasks, EATS WELL, has FUN and ENJOYS LIFE!

- ## ADD LIFE THINGS TO YOUR TO-DO LIST, NOT JUST WORK THINGS!

How about giving the same priority to PLEASURE and RELAXATION as you have to your WORK list?

- ## LEARN TO SAY 'NO'

When you say 'NO' to something you DON'T LIKE or WANT, you're actually saying 'YES' to YOURSELF – you're affirming that you have a RIGHT to DISAGREE with or REFUSE something that is not in your best interest. You are also recognising that your TIME, ENERGY and HEALTH are every bit as IMPORTANT as everyone else's.

- ## LEARN TO DELEGATE

Have you actually ASKED for HELP? People may have got so used to you NOT ASKING, they think you're MANAGING! Your fierce INDEPENDENCE may have sent a message to people that they are not NEEDED, and people LIKE to be NEEDED!

You may be surprised at how willing others may be to help you when you ADMIT that you're STRUGGLING.

- **BE A FRIEND TO YOURSELF**

Would you really put SOMEONE you CARED about through such a PUNISHING ROUTINE?

Start being KINDER to yourself. You have as much RIGHT to be HAPPY, PEACEFUL and able to ENJOY LIFE as anyone else. Why should you be EXEMPT?

And of course ...

- **KNOW WHEN TO STOP!**

But what about that EMPTINESS we talked about before? How do I fill that?

You know what? EMPTINESS is actually SPACE in DISGUISE!

When you LET GO of doing TOO MUCH, you make ROOM for doing JUST ENOUGH!

You now have the SPACE to fill with whatever you have been MISSING!

Book that HOLIDAY! Take that PLEASURE TRIP! Dig in your GARDEN! Do that COURSE! Take up ART! Adopt a PET! Do WHATEVER the hell you actually LIKE!

Haven't you EARNED it?

A word of WARNING: keep an EYE on yourself! It can be way too easy to SLIP BACK into your old habits and, before you KNOW it, you're back in BURNOUT again.

Hopefully, you've LEARNED from this experience and will avoid falling into that trap again.

The WISDOM of BURNOUT

Okay, so you got FRIED from BURNOUT. It felt BAD, didn't it?

Well, why WOULD you? You've BEEN there, you've DONE that and hopefully you've come to REALISE that NOTHING is worth DESTROYING yourself for!

Believe it or not, it's NOT a BAD thing to have reached BURNOUT!

Indeed, BURNOUT can take you to a TOUGH place, but here's the THING – would you have stopped PUSHING so hard OTHERWISE?

Hmmm ... maybe NOT ...

Humans tend to be STUBBORN about making necessary changes until things become too PAINFUL to NOT make them!

Let's be HONEST – you KNEW you were doing TOO MUCH, that you'd taken on MORE than you could HANDLE, that you were feeling UNWELL and EXHAUSTED ... but you pressed on ANYWAY!

What was going to make you stop BEFORE it became TOO MUCH, other than to reach a point where you had NO CHOICE but to STOP?

This takes us back to a key question at the start of this book, which asks:

How do you know when you HAVE reached your LIMIT? Is it when you're EXHAUSTED but CARRY ON? Or when you've reached the point where you simply CAN'T carry on?

The sad fact is that, for people who are inclined to BURN OUT, few are likely to stop before they're FORCED to.

So reaching BURNOUT is the one WAKE-UP CALL they're likely to heed.

Be thankful if you reach BURNOUT before becoming SO ILL that you lose the most important thing of all – your ability to LIVE AND ENJOY YOUR LIFE!

So, you're saying that BURNOUT is actually a BLESSING IN DISGUISE?

YES! For the above reasons but also because if you've REACHED the point of BURNOUT, hopefully you will have gained GREATER CLARITY.

When you have a better UNDERSTANDING of why you were in BURNOUT in the first place, you can take ACTION to IMPROVE your situation – and remember to reach out for HELP if you need it.

Well, you now know:

- What is IMPORTANT

- What MEANS the MOST to you

- What you LOVE and MISS having

- What you DISLIKE and can do WITHOUT

- What is WORTH THE EFFORT and what isn't

- Who will STAND BY YOU

- What is worth FIGHTING FOR

- What you need to RELEASE

- What you need to ACCEPT

- What you STAND for

And, most of ALL – what your BODY, MIND and SPIRIT need most to feel FULLY ALIVE!

Here is a recap of TECHNIQUES to help you AVOID burnout:

- Don't take on TOO MUCH.

- Learn to TRUST yourself to LOOK AFTER yourself.

- Ask for HELP when you need it.

- See life in more POSITIVE terms. It is not meant to be a BATTLE.

- Take care of your PHYSICAL HEALTH.

- Adapt to new SITUATIONS rather than RESISTING change.

- Live in the PRESENT.

- Don't feed your STRESS.

- RESTING is essential to top up the energy you need.

- Doing NOTHING is actually doing SOMETHING (positive).

- Importantly, seek PROFESSIONAL HELP if needed.

And finally, being WISE enough to know when to QUIT is a STRENGTH – not a sign of FAILURE!

GETTING HELP in times of crisis

Emergency Services: 000
triplezero.gov.au

Beyond Blue: 1300 224 636
beyondblue.org.au

Child Protection Victoria: 13 12 78
services.dhhs.vic.gov.au/child-protection

Headspace: 1800 011 511
headspace.org.au
Support for 12- to 25-year-olds

Kids Helpline: 1800 55 1800
kidshelp.com.au
Support for 5- to 25-year-olds

Lifeline: 13 11 14
lifeline.org.au
24-hour crisis counselling

Mensline Australia: 1300 78 99 78
mensline.org.au

National Office for Child Safety:
childsafety.pmc.gov.au

Respect: 1800 737 732
1800respect.org.au
For victims of physical or sexual abuse

Safe Steps Victoria: 1800 015 188
safesteps.org.au
For victims of domestic violence

Suicide Call Back Service: 1300 659 467
suicidecallbackservice.org.au

SuicideLine Victoria: 1300 651 251
suicideline.org.au

Also by
Bev Aisbett ...

CRUISING THROUGH CALAMITY:
Handling anxiety in anxious times

A book for anyone and everyone who finds themselves going through big change, hard times, bad luck or tough sh*t. A book for right now, as it turns out.

Cruising Through Calamity is a much-needed book to help people manage their emotions through challenging times. So whether you're struggling during the pandemic or navigating a personal crisis, if you're feeling anxious or overwhelmed and your emotions are getting the better of you, then this is the book you need right now to help you cruise through calamities, big and small.

Written in Bev Aisbett's clear, simple and straightforward style, using straight talk and humour to defuse, entertain, explain and inform, this is a most timely and topical book to help anyone feeling overwhelmed by uncertainty, difficult feelings and tough circumstances.

ISBN: 978 1 4607 5975 2

WORRY-PROOFING YOUR ANXIOUS CHILD

If your child too often: seeks reassurance, invents illnesses, avoids interactions, avoids trying new things, becomes emotional over minor upsets, or is afraid to sleep alone, reluctant to go to school or scared of numerous things ... then anxiety could be an issue for them.

Commonly, a child experiencing anxiety has self-doubt, lacks confidence and becomes easily overwhelmed. So how do you best help them?

From Bev Aisbett, Australia's bestselling self-help author, *Worry-Proofing Your Anxious Child* is a calm, clear and, above all, reassuring book to help parents (and teachers) of anxious children. Filled with simple explanations and practical advice, this book will assist everyone who wants to help a child overcome their anxieties and learn to live more confidently.

ISBN: 978 1 4607 5719 2

30 DAYS 30 WAYS
TO OVERCOME ANXIETY

From Bev Aisbett, Australia's bestselling anxiety expert and author of the classic national bestseller *Living with IT*, comes a proven and practical workbook to help people manage their anxiety, with simple daily strategies for work and for home.

Based on the exercises Bev has been teaching and writing about for the past twenty years, *30 Days 30 Ways to Overcome Anxiety* provides clear, simple daily building blocks to help people manage their anxiety and assist in recovery.

Designed to be carried in handbags or backpacks as a daily companion, this is a highly approachable, concise, practical and, above all, proven method of overcoming anxiety.

ISBN: 978 1 4607 5465 8

LIVING WITH IT:
A Survivor's Guide to Overcoming Panic & Anxiety

Panic attacks — approximately 5% of the population will experience them at sometime or another. Seemingly coming from nowhere, the dread of having an attack itself transforms the ordinary world of everyday life into a nightmare of anxiety and suffering.

In this refreshing and accessible guide, Bev Aisbett, a survivor herself of Panic Syndrome, tells us how panic disorders develop and how to recognise the symptoms. With the aid of her inimitable cartoons, she covers topics such as changing negative thought patterns, seeking professional help and, ultimately, learning skills for recovery. *Living With IT* provides much needed reassurance and support, leading the way out of the maze of panic with humour and the insight of first-hand experience.

ISBN: 978 1 4607 5717 8

30 DAYS 30 WAYS
TO OVERCOME DEPRESSION

When you're suffering from depression, sometimes it's as much as you can do to get out of bed, let alone read a book. But this just isn't any other book. This is a practical day-by-day workbook, with clear, simple daily building blocks and exercises designed to help pull you out of the inertia of depression. It's a highly approachable, concise and, above all, practical way to help manage depression.

Featuring all-new material from experienced counsellor and bestselling author of the self-help classics *Living with IT* and *Taming the Black Dog*, Bev Aisbett has based this book on many of the exercises she has been teaching and writing about for the past twenty years to help people manage their depression.

ISBN: 978 1 4607 5810 6

TAMING THE BLACK DOG:
A Guide to Overcoming Depression

Don't want to get out of bed in the morning?

Feeling as though the light is fading at
the end of the tunnel?

You may be suffering from depression, a condition
Winston Churchill referred to as the 'Black Dog'.

Now expanded and fully updated, *Taming the Black
Dog* is a simple guide to managing depression, which
an estimated 1 in 5 people will suffer in one form or
another at some time in their lives. Modelled on
Bev Aisbett's successful *Living with IT*, *Taming the
Black Dog* has a unique blend of wit and information,
and is an invaluable guide for both chronic sufferers
of depression as well as anyone with a
fit of 'the blues'.

ISBN: 978 1 4607 5696 6